THE
DIVINE DISCIPLINE
OF ISRAEL

*AN ADDRESS AND THREE LECTURES ON
THE GROWTH OF IDEAS IN THE
OLD TESTAMENT*

BY

G. BUCHANAN GRAY, M.A.
LECTURER IN HEBREW AND OLD TESTAMENT THEOLOGY IN
MANSFIELD COLLEGE, OXFORD

Wipf and Stock Publishers
199 W 8th Ave, Suite 3
Eugene, OR 97401

The Divine Discipline of Israel
An Address and Three Lectures on the Growth of Ideas in the Old Testament
By Gray, George Buchanan
ISBN: 1-59752-152-3
Publication date 4/25/2005
Previously published by Adam and Charles Black, 1900

TO

MY FATHER

AND

MY MOTHER

THIS LITTLE VOLUME IS GRATEFULLY

DEDICATED

PREFACE

THE deepest interest of the Old Testament centres in its ideas; and the surest way to understand those ideas lies through the study of them in their genesis and growth. Such study must share with all others the possibility of uncertainty in detail, and the liability to error. But it is unwise to defer the attempt to understand anything till everything subsidiary to that understanding is certain and beyond dispute.

The address and the lectures of which this volume consists were alike given and are now published in the belief that the readiness to accept the main conclusions of the modern literary criticism of the Old Testament is already sufficiently widespread to justify an exposition and interpretation of the history of some of the Old Testament ideas based on those conclusions, yet without reference to the processes by which they have been reached.

The subject of the lectures is large, and the lectures themselves must be regarded merely as illustrations of it. They are published in accordance with the request of some who heard them. I should have preferred, on many grounds, to have dealt with the subject on a more adequate scale, and in a less fragmentary manner. But for this I have not at present the requisite leisure. And it is not unlikely that those who may care to read the present brief discussion, would have had little inclination to devote time to one that was longer and more elaborate.

The volume will serve its purpose if to some small extent it succeeds in showing how vividly the Old Testament illustrates the fact that men have differed in different ages in their apprehension, and consequently in their expression, of the abiding realities.

G. BUCHANAN GRAY.

MANSFIELD COLLEGE,
OXFORD, *November* 1899.

THE DIVINE DISCIPLINE
OF ISRAEL

A PAPER READ BEFORE

THE CONGREGATIONAL UNION OF ENGLAND AND WALES

AT LEICESTER

ON 1st OCTOBER 1896.

THE
DIVINE DISCIPLINE
OF
ISRAEL

THAT Israel was a chosen people, elected of God for the accomplishment of a particular purpose—the spiritual enlightenment of the nations through the revelation of the true God—is an idea which is deeply rooted in the Scriptures, and which has in manifold ways dominated Christian thought. For the Christian thinker has been quick to trace in the chequered fortunes of the chosen people the consistent working of the Divine mind shaping for itself out of the natural Israel a fit instrument for the fulfilling of its design.

Now during the last century, exploration, linguistic study, critical investigation, and historical research have all contributed data which render the history of Israel a very different story from that which was thus interpreted. Is it, then, still possible to discern in it the discipline of a nation for a Divine purpose? This is the question I propose to raise; and, within the limits of time at my disposal, to throw out suggestions for an answer to it.

In the first place, let me indicate the *general* result of discovery and research. *Generally* speaking, these have brought to light a much greater original likeness between Israel and the neighbouring peoples, and the continuance of much of this likeness to a far later period in the history than was formerly recognised.

So long as our knowledge of other ancient Semitic peoples was based only on the fragmentary and but partly intelligible accounts of the classical authors, Israel appeared all the more peculiar as being the only Semitic people known to us through native sources. But the discovery and interpretation of other native Semitic records quickly brought to light many points of resemblance. Thus it became impossible any longer to hold that a part of Israel's peculiar task was to preserve an account of the origin and early history of the world, so soon as it was seen that that account was derived from Babylon, and consisted not of matters of fact, but of legend and myth. In this particular instance, it is true, comparison has revealed dissimilarity no less than similarity; the Divine revelation of which Israel was the channel is now seen to consist in the spiritual truth which shines through the legend and the myth. Again, the discovery of an important inscription[1] of Israel's near neighbours, the Moabites, showed that there was an even more far-reaching similarity between the religious ideas of Hebrews and Moabites so late as the ninth century—that is to say, down to the early years of Elijah. The Babylonian narratives are distinguished from

[1] A translation of part of this is given in the Appendix, pp. 126–128.

the Hebrew by their polytheistic standpoint; but to the Moabite scribe his god, Chemosh, is scarcely less unique than is Jehovah to the contemporary Hebrew writers. These familiar examples must suffice to illustrate the manner in which the discovery of fresh facts through exploration has stripped many elements in the religion, history, and literature of Israel of their uniqueness and peculiarity. For what has been done in another direction by the study of comparative religion, and especially by the comparative study of Semitic religions, I need only refer to the works[1] of the late Professor Robertson Smith, who has traced many a custom and many a sacrificial rite, which once ranked as the peculiar mark of the Hebrews, to their origin in the customs and religion of the common ancestors of the various Semitic nations.

But if the similarity of the early Hebrews has only recently become clear, the long-recognised peculiarity of the later Hebrews

[1] More especially *The Religion of the Semites*.

or Jews is still an undisputed fact. Nothing has arisen to call in question the unique part the Jews have played in history, nor that that uniqueness consists in their religion. In other words, no new facts, no new theories which those facts have generated, have diminished the importance of the history of Israel; for, together with Greece and Rome, Israel still exercises a mighty influence over the life of to-day. Greece remains none the less supreme in art because discovery and research have shown that the efflorescence of her art, instead of being sudden, was preceded by long ages of growth, and that it owed something to the influence of foreign models; nor Israel in religion, because it can no longer be denied that that religion which has rendered her unique was not the birth of a day, but the slow growth of centuries out of an original common to other peoples. It is the finished product, the culminating point, which in each instance alike establishes the claim to supremacy and gives a consequent importance to the prior history.

While, therefore, the historian to-day has to make clear the extent of the common basis of the religions of Israel and other peoples, a yet more important part of his task is to trace the transition from similarity to dissimilarity, to mark the crises of the history, and to account as best he may for the fact that this people, once merely one of several similar Semitic confederations, came in the course of its history so to diverge from the rest that, while they have passed away leaving behind them little discernible influence, it, through its religion, remains the most potent and beneficent factor in the life of our own times. The Christian thinker, the theologian, has yet another task : accepting the facts, he has to consider their bearing on his conception of God, and then to give them their final interpretation in the light of that conception. In attempting to indicate how that task may be discharged, under the changed circumstances occasioned by fresh knowledge, I must content myself with a single illustration. For this purpose I take the growth of the monotheistic idea or belief. Ultimately the most essential peculiarity of the Hebrew religion in the realm of belief was its monotheism; originally this was not the case; for in common with the neighbouring nations the early Hebrews were not monotheists.

Kuenen, with a true sense of the resemblance of the Hebrew to other Semitic religions, sought the ground of similarity in a common polytheism: as in other countries men worshipped at the same time many gods, so, he argued, David and Saul and other Hebrew leaders worshipped other gods besides Jehovah. Renan, on the other hand, with a keen sense of the supremacy, for example, of Jehovah among the Hebrews, or of Chemosh among the Moabites, propounded his famous theory of a common Semitic monotheism, and argued that Hebrews and other Semites alike were governed by a monotheistic tendency. Further research, greatly stimulated by the writings of both these scholars, has confirmed them in their point of agreement—the similarity of the Hebrews and other Semites, but has corrected both where they disagreed, viz., in the ground of that similarity. The Semites were not monotheists in the sense that they had a common belief in one supreme God of the whole world, nor were David and his contemporaries polytheists in the sense that they worshipped many gods. Polytheism is not the only alternative to monotheism; and the outcome of investigation has been to show that the Hebrews, not excluding the great teachers and leaders down to the eighth century, believed in many gods, but served only one— viz., Jehovah. In other words, they were monolatrists, not monotheists: polytheists in thought, though not in practice. Thus the author of the Decalogue recognises the existence of other gods in the very command in which he enjoins the sole worship of Jehovah; Jephthah sees in Chemosh a god as real as Jehovah, and as capable of giving a land to his worshippers as Jehovah to Israel. David, the devoted servant of Jehovah and famous as fighting the battles of Jehovah, yet looks upon Jehovah as confined to his own land, and therefore regards a decree of banishment as equivalent to being compelled to serve other gods.

It is true that Bæthgen, the author of a comparatively recent work[1] of outstanding merits on Semitic religion, has striven, while granting the correctness of the foregoing statement of early Hebrew thought, to prove the dissimilarity even in this respect of the Hebrews. He argues that the Hebrews, though they believed in many, yet worshipped only one God, and therefore differed from all other Semites, who not only believed in but also worshipped more gods than one. I am convinced that this is unsound. Bæthgen has himself shown the tendency towards simplicity as we follow the stream of Semitic history upwards. Everything goes to indicate that a common stage of religious thought and practice in the particular which I am discussing, through which many, if not all, the Semitic peoples passed, was that in which we

[1] *Beiträge zur semitischen Religionsgeschichte* (1888).

find the Hebrews down to the time of Amos. Others have, with greater reason, sought in a deeper moral conception of their God a difference between the early Hebrews and their neighbours. This I must not discuss;[1] I will only remark that in the present dearth of records of the religious thought of Moabites and similar people, it can be nothing more than an inference from the ultimate diversity of Israel. But whether the inference be correct or not, it does not affect the fact that the Hebrews down to the time of Amos worshipped only one but believed in the existence of many gods; nor does it diminish the extreme probability that in both these respects there was a thorough-going similarity between the Hebrews and their neighbours.

The peculiarity of Israel in these particulars first emerges, strikingly enough, in an act of resistance—in a successful attempt to maintain the existing belief and practice against

[1] See, however, the three lectures which follow, and especially the observations on, and illustrations of, early Hebrew morality on pp. 92–97.

the introduction of others fraught with moral evil; in other words, in the maintenance of the worship of Jehovah only against the attempted introduction of the worship of other gods also. This was the inestimably valuable work of Elijah: Israel under his guidance came to differ from all other Semites by overcoming a temptation to which they yielded. So long as a Semitic people lived a comparatively secluded life, or had intercourse or waged warfare only with other nations of similar beliefs and equal power, there was little temptation to exchange their worship of one God for the worship of many. But as the national life expanded, commercial or diplomatic or political reasons made the transition easy. The commercial Phœnicians were tempted, and very early yielded to the temptation, to add to the worship of their own god that of the peoples with whom they traded; Ahab, having contracted alliance with Tyre by marriage with a Tyrian princess, would, out of diplomatic courtesy, have added to the worship of Jehovah the worship of the

Tyrian god; stricken before the irresistible march of the Assyrian, the peoples of Syria were only too easily led to seek the help of the apparently omnipotent gods of Assyria. This in each case was to follow the line of least resistance. Many in Israel also followed it; but Elijah, Amos, Hosea, Isaiah, and Micah remained firm to the sole worship of Jehovah. How shall we account for this but by the working in these men of the Divine Spirit? For, if we have regard only to so-called natural causes, the line along which they thus led the better part of their people was that of greatest resistance.

Elijah succeeded in maintaining and re-awakening the single-hearted loyalty of the people to Jehovah by mere resistance to an innovation, because nothing had happened which even to the people suggested that Jehovah had forfeited their trust. It was different with the prophets of the eighth century. Up to a certain stage, and under certain conditions, a monolatrous worship is free from the moral imperfections of a polytheistic worship, and practically as effective as monotheism. But the belief in a national god makes that god's first concern his people : if his people suffer temporary defeat he may be merely angry ; but, if they suffer permanent subjection, he is proved impotent, and the people have a right to seek protection from others. It was this very natural line of argument that in the eighth century led many of the Hebrews, and apparently all their near neighbours, to add to their worship of one national god that of other and strange gods. And it was then, also, that the greatest step was taken towards the dissimilation of Israel. It had become impossible on the old monolatrous grounds to explain the course of events consistently with the power of Jehovah. The prophets, therefore, rose above it by insisting that Jehovah's first concern was not Israel but righteousness ; they came to perceive and teach the unity and moral order of the world. The claim of Kuenen that the prophets were the creators of ethical monotheism is therefore (in spite of the criticism it has received) substantially correct. There were, of course, moral elements in the earlier conception of Jehovah, but that is not to the point. It is the prophets who first explicitly teach that the moral is the fundamental element in the personality of Jehovah, and that the guiding principle of His activity is righteousness, and not the interests of a single people. Not to see this is to lose sight of the fact that the growth of the monotheistic idea in Israel is ever along moral rather than speculative lines. It is most significant that Israel passes out of a monolatrous into a monotheistic stage of religion just when the former must otherwise have given place to one which would have involved a lower morality.

In order to illustrate afresh the moral character of the development, let me refer to another movement. Monolatry—the worship of one god—may pass into polytheism either, as we have just seen, by syncretism—*i.e.*, by the addition of fresh objects of worship—or by differentiation—*i.e.*, by dividing the original single object of worship into many. This latter danger in Israel was associated with the high places; here Jehovah was worshipped, probably with an ancient Canaanitish cultus, as the Baal or owner of such and such a place. While the worshippers did not explicitly differentiate Jehovah as the Baal of one place from Jehovah the Baal of another, this differentiation virtually took place; Hosea refuses to identify the popular Baals with Jehovah, and insists that, as a consequence of this worship, Jehovah the national God, the source of righteousness, was regarded as different from the bountiful giver of the fruits of the earth. The moral danger of separating Jehovah, the source of law and justice, from the Baal who gave the gifts of harvest, can easily be seen, and when realized explains the centralization which marked the Deuteronomic reformation. It was on *moral* grounds that the reformers insisted both by word and symbol that " Jehovah our God is one Jehovah." Thus the great keynote even of Deuteronomy is not a speculative monotheism, but the unity of Jehovah, and this is put forward as a reason for living with a single purpose and unmixed love of God.

The advance made by the prophets and the Deuteronomic reformers was secured by the Exile and the Restoration. Certainly these great events have lost nothing by the new setting of the history. In Babylon the people were weaned from their worship at the high places; by the Restoration they were convinced that Jehovah governed the movements of all nations, and not alone of their own. How greatly, rather, has the discipline of the Exile [1] become clearer now that the great prophecy at the end of the book of Isaiah has been placed in its true position! That boundless outlook, that unquenchable faith; those exalted conceptions of the uniqueness, the omniscience, the omnipotence, the tenderness of Jehovah; that inspiring belief in the mission of the suffering people, —these are not the result of a Divine opening of Isaiah's eyes to the affairs of a distant

---

[1] For the influence of the Exile in certain other respects, see below, pp. 86 ff., 115 ff.

century : they are the lessons of the discipline of a nation described, at the very time that he was learning them, by one of its noblest spirits.

The centuries that followed served still further to strengthen and diffuse the lofty conception of God which had now been attained. The dispersion of the Jews in many countries — Babylon, Egypt, Greece, Rome—during this period was preparing the soil for the later preaching of the Gospel. Among the Jews themselves we have been accustomed to discern during the centuries between the Restoration and the time of Christ an almost too great intensification of the transcendental idea of God. No longer as of old can Jehovah be approached in many places where he records His name ; His name is but in one place. He is removed far above men by either priest or law. This period has been regarded as pre-eminently legal, and almost its only purpose, to serve as a dark background to the teaching of Jesus. But critical research, while in one direction it has intensified the legal character of the period, has in another modified it. The post-exilic period was not only the period of the law, but also of the Psalms. For then, to refer only to what is generally admitted, the Psalms were constantly edited and gathered into fresh collections —an indication that they were treasured and influential. Men were, therefore, not only taught through the law the exaltation and holiness and uniqueness of God, but through the Psalms learnt to hold personal communion with Him. Thus was the way prepared for the final revelation of God in the Incarnation; among a people whose belief in the unity and uniqueness of God had through the discipline of these last centuries become so intense, the final truths of the manifoldness of God and of man's divine nature could be safely unfolded without danger of a divided worship and a divided moral allegiance.

With this I bring to an end this necessarily very inadequate sketch of the growth of the monotheistic idea. But I hope I have been able to make clear that the reconstruction of the history has, in many important respects, increased rather than diminished the evidence for a divine discipline of Israel. We have lost, it is true, all ground for accepting as historical fact the revelation of an elaborate ritual at Sinai; but we have gained insight into the real work of the prophets, and, may I not add, a firmer conviction, if a less mechanical conception, of the working in them of the spirit of God. We see them standing at the parting of the ways when two courses alone were possible—an upward and a downward; we see many of their countrymen, all their Semitic neighbours, taking the easy downward path to polytheism with all its moral confusion; and we see the prophets leading a spiritual nucleus of their nation amid the difficulties and confusion of the time, upward to a loftier and sublimer faith in the moral unity of the universe and the righteousness of God. Surely to those who hold that God takes greater pleasure in the rightness of a man's conduct than in the correctness of his ritual, this exchange must be welcome.

Less welcome, no doubt, because less immediately explicable, will be the manner in which I have described the early Hebrew conception of Jehovah. And yet it is, I am convinced, a perfectly well-established fact that the early Hebrews believed that many gods existed, and that by their existence the power of Jehovah was limited; I am also convinced that the attempt to make Moses, and David, and others, exceptions to this rule has broken down. I will, in conclusion, offer, though with all diffidence, one or two suggestions as to the meaning of this fact.

Christian theology has always had to take account of the fact that the final and complete revelation in Jesus Christ was preceded by centuries of incomplete revelation. Nor has it found it in any way impossible to understand and interpret this fact. But if the perfect revelation in Jesus Christ was preceded by the imperfect revelation through the prophets, there can surely be nothing inexplicable in the prophetic revelation having itself been preceded by a yet more imperfect stage such as I have indicated; in other words, there is no incongruity between the fact that, to cite a single name, Moses believed in the existence of many gods, and the belief that he was a vehicle of revelation. The belief underlying monolatry is the partial perception of monotheism, just as simple monotheism is the partial perception of the manifold monotheism of the Christian faith. Monolatry is not practically false; and under certain circumstances, to which I have already alluded, and in which the early Hebrews lived, it is morally as effective as monotheism. It is, therefore, wholly different in character from polytheism, which is practically as well as speculatively false.

But there is a further question which all those will ask who see in the history of Israel the Divine discipline of a nation—viz., What purpose was served by this monolatrous stage in revelation? This would, I imagine, be satisfactorily answered if we could point to valuable elements in the later idea of, or belief in God, which were derived from this early period. But may we not trace back to it the intensity of the belief, and the sense, if I may so phrase it, of a personal and peculiar interest in God? There can scarcely be a doubt that intensity was gained by limitation; that the early Hebrew sense of Jehovah was deeper from the fact that He was their God alone, maintaining their cause against rival nations and rival gods. Through these centuries of monolatry the personality and complete reality of Jehovah became so graven in the national consciousness, that when in due time the higher and fuller idea of Jehovah was reached, it was reached without loss of the life-giving elements in the earlier and narrower conception. When Israel no longer believed that Jehovah was one of many gods, nor God alone of Israel, it could yet say Jehovah is my shepherd, my portion. In other words, the very phrases and thoughts that spring naturally out of the earlier are still necessary for the full expression of the later and higher conception. How great a part the Psalms have played in intensifying and making effective the religious consciousness of all generations, who shall say ? And yet is it not reasonable to assert that without that earlier national discipline they would never have gained that power which they possess.

I have throughout this paper intentionally avoided all attempts to prove the facts to which I have referred. Many have been disputed, some are still. But I am hopeful that in devoting my whole time to the presentation and interpretation of them, I have adopted the course most likely to initiate a discussion which may requicken for us a belief which has won the attention in former ages of the Church of her most illustrious thinkers, and which has been one of the greatest factors in giving breadth and grandeur to Christian thought and Christian culture.

THE GROWTH OF MORAL IDEAS

IN THE

OLD TESTAMENT

THREE LECTURES DELIVERED TO
THE FRIENDS' SUMMER SCHOOL OF THEOLOGY
AT BIRMINGHAM
ON 11TH, 12TH, AND 13TH SEPTEMBER 1899

THE
GROWTH OF MORAL IDEAS

IN THE

OLD TESTAMENT

I

INTRODUCTORY—THE DIVINE MORALITY

For good or evil, directly or indirectly, the Bible has exercised a supreme influence over the moral ideas and the moral conduct of Christian societies. Its influence has been most powerful and most direct where, as in Protestant countries, it has been in the hands of the people, and not simply imparted to them with an authoritative interpretation; and at times when a theory of scriptural infallibility has prevailed. At such times whatever happens to be directly commanded or prohibited in the Bible tends to become earnestly striven for or avoided; and whatever was done by eminent and, in general, praiseworthy individuals whose doings are recorded in the Old Testament, has been apt to call forth a ready, though often a very immoral, defence.

In consequence, the moral influence of the Bible, great and powerful as it has been for good, has not been unmixed. To take a single illustration: the crusade undertaken for the abolition of slavery met with an opposition made all the more stubborn because the laws of the Old Testament, and the examples of its heroes, could be cited in favour of the institution.

This abuse of the Bible cannot, of course, be fairly made a charge against the Bible itself. But the very power of the Bible for good, when rightly used and rightly interpreted, renders any wrong use or interpretation of it correspondingly mischievous. And one of the most mischievous misuses of it is to regard it, in all its parts and all its judgments, as an absolute and final arbiter in matters of morality. The best corrective for this particular misuse is to realize through systematic study that the morality of the Bible is progressive; that its moral ideals change with the progress of time; and that, in consequence, the laws in which those ideals express themselves vary to the extent, in some cases, of direct contradiction.

The subject, then, which lies before us has a very practical bearing; for while, in its extreme forms, the doctrine of the Bible, out of which springs the misuse to which I have referred, is obsolete, its influence still lingers, affecting us often almost unconsciously. But it must suffice merely to indicate this practical bearing of the subject. The present treatment of it is intended to be primarily historical.

Our purpose is to examine, though of necessity very incompletely, the moral ideas of the Hebrews, to discover that course of conduct which appeared to them best, the motives with which they pursued it, and the changes through which both ideas and practice passed in the course of history.

But in the first place a few words must be said with regard to the limitations under which such a study can alone be pursued.

The moral ideas of an age can only be satisfactorily discovered by means of contemporary evidence, and more especially the evidence of contemporary literature. I must here assume, what on a former occasion[1] I endeavoured to prove, that Hebrew literature earlier than the ninth or tenth centuries B.C. exists only in the most meagre fragments, the most notable among these being the song of Deborah. Of Hebrew moral ideas and practice prior to that period our knowledge must be to a large extent inferential—deduced in part from what we know to have been the ideas

[1] In a course of lectures delivered to the Friends' Summer School at Scarborough in August 1897. A fairly full summary of these lectures appeared in *The Friend* of Sept. 3rd, 10th, and 17th, 1897. But the reader who wishes to appreciate the reasons for the literary conclusions which the following lectures assume, should turn to Professor Driver's *Introduction to Old Testament Literature.*

of the Hebrews later, in part from the ideas of kindred peoples in a similar political condition.

But when we come to the earlier periods of extant Hebrew literature—the tenth, ninth, or eighth centuries B.C.—there is still need of caution. Our literary material is still comparatively small in extent, and is in the main of one type—it is the product of prophetic circles. What we directly obtain, therefore, is the moral ideals of the prophets; indirectly we sometimes glean facts relative to the popular ideals, which were in some cases very different from the prophetic. The same statement is largely true of the literature of the seventh century, though in the case of Deuteronomy we have the combined product of priest and prophet, and the fusion, in so far as they were distinct, of the ideas of these two classes. In much of the literature of the post-exilic period the priestly ideals predominate.

Again, if we turn from ideal and theory to practice, there is also need of caution in drawing our conclusions. The literature, as we have seen, is largely prophetic; but the prophets were moral censors. It is necessary to bear this in mind, and so to allow for the fact that our evidence is to a large extent one-sided.

There scarcely exist, therefore, sufficient data to enable us to trace in detail, and at the same time with certainty, the growth of many individual moral ideas, and the extent to which they were realized at different times in the life of the people. We must be content, at any rate on the present occasion, with what is possible without discussing the more obscure and uncertain details of the subject—the study of some of the leading and influential ideas, and the observation of certain great and far-reaching changes.

There is one outstanding characteristic of Hebrew morality which must be considered at the outset. It is, if I am not mistaken, the most effective cause of the influence of Hebrew moral ideas. I refer to the close relation between Hebrew theology and Hebrew morality. This connection is far from necessary. Among the Greeks theology was not less strikingly divorced from morality than among

THE GROWTH OF MORAL IDEAS 41

the Hebrews it was conjoined with it. The Greek gods were notorious for conduct which, when practised by men, called forth severe moral reprobation. In a word, the Greek gods were immoral, and judged to be immoral by their worshippers. We may, it is true, find incompletely ethical elements in the early Hebrew conception of Jehovah; but Jehovah never by His conduct offended the moral consciousness of His worshippers. He demanded by His example a standard of life in men higher than that which was prevalent; He never by His conduct excused in men what was lower than the standard of the time.

Closely connected with this fact is another. It is characteristic of the Hebrew teachers that the divine conduct and nature become the ideal for man, for the Hebrew at least, to aim at. The saying " Ye shall be holy; for I, Jehovah, your God, am holy," is indeed the utterance of a comparatively late code of laws;[1] and " the righteous Jehovah loveth

[1] Lev. xix. 2 belongs to a code (known as the 'Law of Holiness'), drawn up in the early part of the sixth century B.C.

righteousness"[1] of a post-exilic psalmist; but the principle these sayings inculcate is certainly as old as the earliest literary prophets. The burden of the preaching of Amos was this—Israel chosen by Jehovah for special intimacy with himself must perish and surrender this intimacy, because it has failed to show that righteous conduct which can alone maintain such intimacy.[2]

Morality thus acquired among the Hebrews all the force and power of a personalized ideal. Morality was no abstract matter appealing only to the cultured and trained intellect; it appealed to men at large, being strengthened by its union with religious emotion. To the Greeks the gods, regarded as often immoral in their conduct, were ideals of the human form; and Greece has handed down to all time the standard of beauty, and done more than any nation to inspire men with the sense of it. To the Hebrews, God was the ideal of human conduct and human character; and if the Hebrews have not given to men

[1] Psalm xi. 7.   [2] See especially Amos iii. 2.

ideals of life nobler and loftier than those of some of the sages of Greece and Rome, they have certainly inspired a more general and a deeper passion for morality.

I intend to bring before you the subject of Hebrew moral ideas, so far as time will permit, by means of three discussions. We have just seen how closely related are the theology and the morality of the Hebrews, and how powerful an influence was exercised by their conception of God over the moral ideas and practice of the Hebrews. In the first place, therefore, we will consider the morality of Jehovah as it appears in the Old Testament, especially in its relation to human conduct; next we will examine the growth of the sense of individual responsibility, and glance at some Hebrew and Jewish ideals of conduct; and thirdly, we will observe the deepening of the motive of conduct.

THE DIVINE MORALITY, ESPECIALLY IN ITS RELATION TO HUMAN CONDUCT

The most important elements in the Hebrew conceptions on this subject will come to light as we seek answers to three questions: (1) How was Jehovah related to mankind at large? (2) What did the Hebrews mean by holiness? (3) What did they understand by righteousness?

(1) The early faith of Israel has been accurately and succinctly expressed in the phrase—Jehovah was the God of Israel, and Israel was the people of Jehovah. In a word, Jehovah was a national God, demanding homage from His people who were to have no other gods before Him—*i.e.*, in His presence or beside Him—expecting homage from no other people; in return for the loyalty of His people Jehovah fights their battles (the battles of Israel are "battles of Jehovah"[1]) and maintains them in possession of the land in which He had

[1] Num. xxi. 14; 1 Sam. xxv. 28; the phrase in the original is the same in both passages.

THE GROWTH OF MORAL IDEAS 45

settled them. He is fitly worshipped only in the land which could indifferently be termed after its immediate owner, 'the land of Jehovah,' or after its sub-owners, the land of Israel.[1] Other lands, as the property of other gods, are 'unclean' from the point of view of Jehovah and Israel; food eaten in them, since it cannot be properly rendered fit for use by the appropriate religious rites, is unclean food.[2] Exiles from the land of Jehovah can no longer worship Him; and an army of Hebrews fighting beyond the borders of their country is apt to be discomfited by the wrath of the god of the land.[3]

Jehovah's interests, then, are limited to Israel; Israel's worship and allegiance to Jehovah. Jehovah is especially Israel's champion in battle; but He is also the source of Israel's law and the patron of justice within Israel. It is the statutes of Jehovah

---

[1] See, *e.g.*, Hos. ix. 3. [2] Hos. ix. 3 f.; Am. vii. 17.
[3] 1 Sam. xxvi. 19; 2 Kings iii. 27; *cf.* 2 Kings v. 17. For the national conception of Jehovah, see also Judges xi. 12-28; for similar national conceptions of Chemosh, god of Moab, see the inscription of Mesha, especially the passage quoted in the Appendix, pp. 126-128.

that the Hebrew law-givers give to the people; the decisions of Jehovah that their priests and prophets obtain for them.[1]

The consequence of this national conception of Jehovah was that there was no religious and moral bond regulating the conduct of the Hebrews with men of other nations. Conduct, which between fellow-Hebrews was offensive in Jehovah's eyes, was inoffensive when practised by a Hebrew towards one who was not a Hebrew. For example, the exaction of interest on money lent was considered by the Hebrews, as indeed also by the ancient Greeks and Romans, to be an injury to the debtors, and was consequently forbidden. " If thou lend money," so runs the ancient Hebrew law as it stands in a code of the eighth century B.C., " to any of My people with thee that is poor, thou shalt not be to him as a creditor; neither shall ye lay interest upon him."[2]

[1] *Cf.* especially Ex. xviii. 12 ff.

[2] Ex. xxii. 25 ; *cf.*, in the Law of Holiness (a code of the sixth century B.C.), Lev. xxv. 35–37. The Revised Version misleadingly retains the term 'usury'; in modern English 'interest' is the true equivalent of the Hebrew term. The law forbids not merely exorbitant interest, but interest altogether.

But the prohibition is strictly limited to dealings between Hebrews and Hebrews; the Deuteronomic law (seventh century B.C.) is explicit on the point—" Thou shalt not make thy neighbour, *i.e.*, thy fellow Hebrew, give interest; . . . but a foreigner thou mayest make give interest." [1]

There are, it is true, one or two passages that may seem to the English reader directly to condemn this limitation of moral obligation to fellow-countrymen. Perhaps it is hardly necessary to point out that the 'neighbour' who is mentioned in Lev. xix. 18 is of necessity a fellow-countryman, and that the term is not to be interpreted, historically, as it is interpreted in the parable of the good Samaritan; the contrast makes the point quite clear— " Thou shalt not take vengeance, nor bear any grudge against the children of My people, but thou shalt love thy neighbour as thyself." But in another passage [2] the English translation is more deceptive—" Ye shall have one manner of law, as well for the *stranger* as for

---

[1] Deut. xxiii. 19 f. [2] Lev. xxiv. 22.

the home-born ;" for the term *gēr* here used for stranger is quite distinct from that translated above foreigner (*nokrî*). *Gēr* has a clearly defined significance, and means a person of another tribe or nation settled in Israel and enjoying certain privileges and rights of protection. The stranger or *gēr* is no mere foreigner, and the law has no reference to the conduct of Hebrews towards foreigners with whom they were brought into temporary relation.

Of the change in the significance of the term *gēr* and in the status of the persons so defined, I shall have something more to say. But first let us see how the general ethical limitation which we are now considering illustrates, and is illustrated by, certain familiar incidents.

Jehovah is the God of Israel and the patron of justice within Israel; the Hebrews consequently were bound by moral obligation and the sanction of religion in their dealings with one another, but were entirely free of these in their dealings with foreigners. In the latter case they were governed purely by considerations of expediency. This ethical limitation is the real explanation of the 'spoiling of the Egyptian,' on which so much apologetic ingenuity has been mis-spent. Had the Hebrews treated their fellow-countrymen as they treated the Egyptians, they would have offended against the moral standard of their time. But since it was foreigners whom they 'spoiled,' they did not. Again, in the story of Abraham's lie to Abimelech,[1] it is Abraham who, judged by our moral standard, deserved punishment; but according to the contemporary Hebrew moral standard, Abraham had committed no sin, for he was under no moral obligation to the foreigner Abimelech. Consequently Abimelech and his servants who had offended quite unwittingly are plagued, while Abraham is not only left untouched, but by his prayers is the means of releasing Abimelech from his sufferings. In Abimelech's reproach, "Thou hast done deeds unto me that ought not to be done," we may probably observe a growing sense that certain conduct was open to reprehension even when practised

[1] Gen. xx.

towards foreigners; but the whole spirit of the narrative is only intelligible when we remember that moral obligation was only strongly felt in the case of one's countrymen.

In this limited range of moral obligation there is nothing peculiar to the Hebrews; it was equally characteristic of early Greek and Roman morality; indeed the Greeks and Romans, as we may see in the teaching of their most eminent moralists, were considerably later than the Hebrews in extending moral obligation beyond the limits of the nation. In the fourth century B.C. Aristotle taught that "Greeks had no more duties to barbarians than to wild beasts," though it is true that Socrates, a century earlier, had proclaimed himself a citizen of the world, and the Greek language had already coined the term 'philanthropy.' Again, it is not till about the period of the rise of Christianity that the Romans, under the influence of Stoical teaching, experienced that "enlargement of moral sympathies, which having at first comprised only a class or a nation, came at last, by the destruction of many artificial barriers, to include all classes and all nations."[1]

In the case of the Hebrews the transcendence of this early limitation was achieved in the first instance in the theological sphere, and was due to the prophets. Face to face with the approaching destruction of Israel by the Assyrian power, the prophets had two alternatives: to infer in common with their contemporaries, and according to the natural logic of then prevalent religious thought, that Jehovah was impotent, or at least inferior in power to the gods of Assyria; or to insist on a new doctrine which at once enhanced the power of Jehovah, and profoundly modified the conception of the manner in which, and the purposes for which, He manifested it. It was, as we are well aware, the latter alternative that the prophets actually took. They taught that Jehovah has power over all nations of the world as well as over Israel,

[1] Lecky's *History of European Morals* (Cabinet Edition), vol. i. pp. 227 ff.

and that He guides the movements of history; but that He exercised this great power in the interests of the righteous government of the world at large, and not merely in the interests of Israel's material wellbeing. This is perhaps the most momentous change to be marked in the history of Old Testament moral ideas; and its full effect was only worked out in the course of centuries. On the one hand it clearly and decisively brought into relief the moral as the essential element in the divine nature; Jehovah's action was seen to be governed by moral ends, not by racial preferences. On the other hand it broke down the sharp distinctions between nation and nation. If Jehovah had ceased to be the God of Israel alone and was felt to be interested in other nations as well as in Israel, it was only a matter of time for the conviction to grow up that he demanded conduct between different nations and between men of different nations similar to that which he had always demanded between Hebrew and Hebrew. But a matter of time unquestionably it was. The full implications of a new doctrine are only gradually perceived.

It is a question which we have no sufficient means to decide, whether even Amos himself clearly saw the full effect on human conduct of his larger conception of Jehovah's morality. How, for instance, would he have felt bound to conduct himself towards a foreigner? Would he have felt it wrong, following the example of Abraham in the story, to deceive a foreigner for his own advantage and convenience? We cannot say. But it is certainly remarkable that the prophet who taught men to enlarge their conception of Jehovah's interest, finds the cause of the doom which is to fall on the various nations in their inhumanity. " It is plain that the sins for which Damascus, Ammon, Moab, and the rest are judged cannot be offences against Jehovah, as the national God of Israel. Amos teaches that heathen nations are to be judged, not because they do not worship Israel's God, but because they have broken the laws of universal morality. The crime of Damascus and Ammon is their inhuman treatment of the Gileadites; the Phœnicians and Philistines are condemned for the barbarous slave trade, fed by kidnapping expeditions, of which Tyre and Gaza were the emporia. In the case of Tyre this offence is aggravated by the fact that the captives were carried off in defiance of the ancient brotherly alliance between Israel and the Phœnician city; and in like manner the sin of Edom is the unrelenting blood-feud with which he follows his brother of Judah. These are the common barbarities and treacheries of Semitic warfare; and it is as such that they are condemned, and not simply because in each case it is Israel that has suffered from them. Moab is equally condemned for a sin that has nothing to do with Israel, but was a breach of the most sacred feelings of ancient piety—the violation of the bones of the king of Edom."[1]

Now Amos here deals with definite concrete cases; he formulates no general principle. We are not justified in inferring, therefore,

[1] W. R. Smith's *The Prophets of Israel* (2nd ed.), pp. 134 f.

that he had reached a belief in 'universal morality,' or that he would have laid down the principle—Jehovah requires that every Hebrew should be under the same moral obligation to any man of any other nation that he is under towards a fellow Hebrew. As a matter of fact all the nations concerned were regarded as closely akin; in a certain sense they were brothers one of another; the Tyrians, as the prophet expresses it, had not remembered 'the brothers' covenant' existing between the Edomites and themselves. But there seems no doubt that the prophet would have condemned the conduct of David when he placed his Ammonite captives "under saws and under harrows of iron and under axes of iron, and made them pass through the brick-kiln."[1]

Amos, therefore, so far, at least, felt the significance of Jehovah's interest in other nations besides Israel that he directly transcended in his teaching the prevalent view that the moral obligation of the Hebrew was limited to his fellow Hebrew.

[1] 2 Sam. xii. 31.

Probably a perfectly distinct perception of the claims of 'universal morality' was not reached by the Jews within the period of the Old Testament. Certainly it was not immediately and generally recognized. For the Deuteronomic Law, which was published some four or five generations after the lifetime of Amos, definitely permits the exaction of interest from foreigners, though the law-givers, regarding the practice as injurious, forbid it in the case of Hebrews. But the principle of universal morality was implicit in the new doctrine of God, and did not remain without effect on conduct.

It is impossible to enter here into a detailed examination of its influence. But its limitations may be illustrated by the change in the character of the strangers or *gērîm*. In early Israel the *gēr* was a person of another tribe or nation enjoying, as distinguished from the mere foreigner (*nokrî*), certain social privileges and a certain protection, but he was still sharply distinguished from the genuine Hebrew in his religious duties and privileges.

He might, for example, eat "that which dieth of itself," though this was strictly forbidden on religious grounds to the Hebrews.[1] In course of time the assimilation of the *gēr* to the Hebrew in matters of religion became increasingly close; until at last the religious rights and duties of both were practically identical.[2] This may be gathered from repeated statements in the priestly code, especially in its secondary or later sections, that "ye shall have one law for the home-born and the stranger."[3] Ultimately the term denotes any full adherent of the Jewish religion who was not of Jewish origin. What was originally a political has become a purely religious term. The *gēr* in the latest Old Testament and subsequent Jewish literature is the term for the proselyte. It has come to denote one who seeks union with the Jews in religion, whereas formerly it denoted one who sought union with them in social life.

Now this is significant enough. Under

[1] Deut. xiv. 21.
[2] Contrast, *e.g.*, the later law of Lev. xvii. 15 with Deut. xiv. 21.
[3] *E.g.*, Exod. xii. 49; Lev. xxiv. 22; Num. ix. 14, xv. 15.

the influence of prophetic teaching the Jews extended the feeling of moral obligation beyond the limits of the Jewish race, but they limited it in its completeness to members of the Jewish religion. Jehovah was more than God of the Jewish *race*; but He remains the God of members of the Jewish religion. Foreigners are no longer excluded from Jehovah's care; but in order to enjoy it they must enter into relation with the Jews. This limitation really marks most of the apparently universalistic visions of the prophets. The nations are to enjoy the privileges of the Messianic age, yet in order to do so they must go up to Zion.[1] In a word, the borders of Israel may be indefinitely enlarged to receive all who are willing to enter, but it is Israel still that is the peculiar care of Jehovah.

(2) THE HOLINESS OF JEHOVAH AND MAN

The fundamental meaning of the root ($kd\check{s}$) from which the words in Hebrew

---

[1] *E.g.*, Isa. ii. 2-4.

denoting holy, holiness, and the like are derived, appears to be that of 'separation,' as this is certainly the meaning of a root of kindred significance which is used alike in Hebrew and Arabic, and through the latter has passed into English in the word *harem* —the quarters in a house separated off for the women.

Holiness is by no means a conception peculiar to the Hebrews. The Phœnicians not less than the Hebrews termed their gods 'holy.' This fact is important. The term in Hebrew remains to the end one of somewhat mixed, and, to our thinking, incongruous meanings. This is due to the fact that in the Old Testament the earliest meanings of the term and the conceptions expressed by them were never wholly cast off.

In the first instance it must be observed that the term holy is far from being a purely ethical term. Things as well as persons may be holy; and it often happened that persons quite accidentally, involuntarily, or even against their will contracted holiness.[1] 'Holiness' was more easily 'caught' than a contagious or infectious disease. How far removed a 'holy' person might be from what we regard as moral may be most strikingly seen in the use of the term 'holy ones' for those who gave themselves up to licentious practices in connection with divine worship.

But while, as I have said, the term never becomes purely moral in the Old Testament, the manner in which it acquires a considerable ethical connotation strikingly illustrates the growth of moral ideas.

Holy things or seasons are an antithesis to 'common' things or seasons. That which is common is open to use without restriction; that which is holy is open to use only under certain conditions. On holy ground Moses must take off his shoes; on the Sabbath, as the holy day, men must abstain from ordinary occupations.

In its application to Jehovah 'holiness'

[1] See, *e.g.*, Lev. vi. 18, 27; and further, W. R. Smith's *Religion of the Semites*, pp. 431 ff.

means in the first instance his 'separation,' 'distinction' from men. It expresses, in a word, divinity with all its peculiar attributes. How far it was ethical depends, therefore, on how far Jehovah was regarded as a moral being. At times Jehovah's holiness seems to be particularly His awful power;[1] in this there is, of course, nothing peculiarly moral. Closely allied with this is the unethical conception of the Divine anger as an almost mechanical reaction against involuntary or well-meaning approach to Him or to things and precincts sacred to Him.[2]

But at other times, and especially with the prophets, the holiness of Jehovah gains a large degree of ethical import. This is nowhere better seen than in the account of Isaiah's vision. The prophet's immediate thought, on perceiving that he is in the holy presence of Jehovah, is that his own iniquity and the iniquity of his people offend that holiness; it is only when his iniquity is

[1] 1 Sam. vi. 20 ; Isa. viii. 13.
[2] 1 Sam. vi. 19 ; 2 Sam. vi. 1 ff; Num. i. 53.

purged away that he can volunteer for the service of the Holy One of Israel.[1]

The same incompatibility between Israel's iniquity and Jehovah's holiness is clearly implied in other parts of the prophet's writings; as, for example, in his address to Israel: "Ah, sinful nation, a people laden with iniquity, a seed of evil-doers, children that deal corruptly. They have forsaken Jehovah, they have despised the Holy One of Israel, they are estranged (and gone) backward." [2]

It may appear strange, and an instance of retrogression in moral ideas, when we find that in the priestly parts of the Hexateuch, though they are so much later in date than Isaiah, the ethical meaning of the term is much less apparent. Holiness in these writings is physical rather than moral; it is contagious. And severe, even fatal punishment, falls on those who offend Jehovah's holiness, not by some moral offence, but by the transgression of some ritual regulation or undue approach

[1] Isa. vi.   [2] Isa. i. 4.

to the sacred precincts. It must be admitted that retrogression as well as progress is certainly possible, and that it is probable that many of the later priestly writers associated morality with holiness less intimately than Isaiah. But it would be easy to do these writers less than justice. It would, for instance, be quite unfair to infer from the literature which they have left us that they had no moral conception of Jehovah in relation to the conduct he required from men. For it must be remembered that the main subject of their laws is ritual, and that they have, in consequence, less occasion for letting us see their distinctly moral ideals. In the closing section of the book of Ezekiel (chaps. xl.–xlviii.) the same physical conception of holiness is also prominent; but we learn from other parts of the same book that the prophet's ideal of conduct included much more than the preservation of such holiness as this. It is only reasonable to infer that the same was true of the priestly writers.

Again, if the severity with which the violation of this physical holiness is punished seems extreme and incompatible with a high morality, it must be remembered that this severity is only part of the general rigour that marked post-exilic Judaism. A parallel may help us to judge fairly. Many of the regulations for the observance of the Sabbath which were enforced by the Puritans were not in themselves of any special moral value, yet the violation of them was punished with severity. It by no means follows that Puritan morality was not lofty. On the other hand, the very severity with which actions then, but now no longer, regarded as immoral, were punished, was but the necessary outcome of that strenuousness of life and that firm adherence to principle which were peculiarly characteristic of the Puritans.

Still, when every allowance has been made, it is true that as long as ritual offences were regarded as of such extreme gravity, a *purely* moral conception of holiness was impossible. The result of the stress laid by post-exilic

THE GROWTH OF MORAL IDEAS 65

Judaism on ritual was unquestionably serious. It kept the conception of sin morally confused. Unintentional pollution of what was holy was sin just as much as an intentional moral offence.

On the other hand we can clearly see that 'holiness' in man included the performance of certain moral duties. This manifestly follows from some of the contexts in which the saying "Ye shall be holy, for I am holy," occurs.[1] Much more significant are the qualifications for dwelling in Jehovah's 'holy' hill specified by a Psalmist of the same period:

"Jehovah . . . who shall dwell in Thy holy hill?
He that walketh uprightly, and worketh righteousness,
And speaketh truth in his heart.
He that slandereth not with his tongue,
Nor doeth evil to his friend,
Nor taketh up a reproach against his neighbour.
In whose eyes a reprobate is despised;
But he honoureth them that fear Jehovah.
He that sweareth to his own hurt, and changeth not.
He that putteth not out his money to interest,
Nor taketh reward against the innocent."[2]

The subject of the divine or of human

[1] Lev. xix. 2; xx. 7.   [2] Ps. xv.; cf. xxiv. 3–5.

holiness is very large, and in many details obscure and incapable of succinct statement. But enough has perhaps been said to show that a term, at first entirely unethical, becomes in the course of history enriched with moral elements. In conclusion, I will cite Mr Skinner's admirable summary of the subject: "From a theological point of view, the chief interest of the O[ld] T[estament] doctrine of holiness lies in this progressive spiritualizing of the idea under the influence of an expanding revelation of God. Although the various steps of the process are obscure, the fact is certain that holiness did come to be conceived more and more as a moral quality. It is probable that the ethical aspect was first introduced in the application of the term to God, and thence transferred to the holiness He requires in his worshippers. In the O[ld] T[estament] the development is arrested at a certain stage, because of the material associations with which the use of the word was invested. One step remained to be taken in order to reach the full Christian sense of holiness, and that was the abrogation of the ceremonial as a term of fellowship with God. When our Lord enunciated the principle that a man is defiled, not by what enters into him, but by what comes out of him, He raised religion to a new level, and made it possible to liberate the moral essence of holiness from the imperfections which clung to it throughout the older dispensation." [1]

(3) THE RIGHTEOUSNESS OF JEHOVAH AND MEN

The original, etymological sense of 'righteousness,' like that of 'holiness,' is obscure. But a starting-point for most of the meanings of the term as actually used, or a general idea under which they may be subsumed, is that of correspondence to a norm or standard. Thus 'just' or 'righteous weights' [2] are standard weights; the man who is, judicially, righteous, *i.e.*, innocent or in the right in a

[1] Hastings' *Dictionary of the Bible*, art. "Holiness."
[2] Lev. xix. 36.

particular matter, is one whose conduct in the case in question has conformed to the standard of law or custom; righteous speech is speech which corresponds to the facts described[1]—a Hebrew mode of expressing 'truth' for which the language, at least in its earlier stages, possessed no very distinctive term.

The term 'righteousness' as an ethical one, is, it will be thus seen, very elastic. Everything depends on the conception of the standard which determines whether conduct and character is righteous enough.

In their earliest usages the various words (nouns, adjectives, and verbs) had, at least predominantly, a forensic sense. They do not refer to character and conduct in general, but to specific acts. Here the standard was clear and fixed; it was that of law or custom.

There are not a few passages in the English Bible in which the rendering of these forensic terms by words of such general ethical import as 'righteous,' 'righteousness,' has obscured, or even perverted, the sense of the original.

[1] Ps. lii. 3.

For example, the Hebrew judges were not instructed to decide the rights of two parties in a dispute out of regard to the whole character of each; but they were to "pronounce him that was in the right" in the particular matter under dispute "to be in the right, and him that was in the wrong to be in the wrong."[1] Bribes were forbidden, because they were apt to deprive a man of the verdict to which he had a right;[2] they induced the judge who was bribed to pronounce him that was in the wrong to be in the right, and to deprive the innocent man of his verdict of acquittal.[3]

The forensic use of the terms in question is particularly characteristic of the earlier Old Testament literature, though it was never discarded. But it becomes, comparatively speaking, less common in the later literature; for it is these terms that the language very naturally employed—and more and more in course of time—to express the very different and larger conception of righteousness of

[1] Deut. xxv. 1.   [2] Exod. xxiii. 8.   [3] Isa. v. 23.

conduct, character, life as a whole, that was excellent and approved.

This fuller, this more generally ethical use of the terms is particularly obvious in the Psalms. The parallelism of Hebrew poetry is in this case, as so often, a great means of interpretation. The synonymous or antithetical terms which appear in the parallel lines show how general the words 'righteous' and the like have become. For example:—

"Therefore the wicked shall not stand in the judgment,
Nor sinners in the congregation of the righteous.
For Jehovah knoweth the way of the righteous;
But the way of the wicked shall perish." [1]

"The wicked plotteth against the righteous." [2]

"The eyes of Jehovah are towards the righteous. . . .
The face of Jehovah is against them that do evil." [3]

"Be glad in Jehovah, and rejoice, ye righteous :
And shout for joy, all ye that are upright in heart." [4]

Nothing, again, but this larger and fuller meaning of righteousness satisfies the require-

[1] Ps. i. 5–6 ; cf. cxl. 11–13. [2] Ps. xxxvii. 12.
[3] Ps. xxxiv. 15 f.
[4] Ps. xxxii. 11 ; cf. xxxiii. 1, lxiv. 10, xcvii. 11, cxxv. 3–5.

ments of the context in the well-known passage, "By his knowledge shall my righteous servant make many righteous."[1]

Now what was that more exact standard which had to be adhered to before any one could be pronounced righteous in this larger sense? In the present instance, we may conveniently consider the case of human righteousness first. And here the standard is obvious: it is the will of God as expressed in the utterances of priests or prophets and, at a later period, especially as expressed in the written law.[2] The Hebrews were not given to philosophical speculation and the analysis of philosophical ideas. Consequently the question which has been so much debated —viz., whether a thing is right because God wills it, or whether God wills it because it is right, scarcely presented itself to them in this sharply-defined form. Certainly, in general, the Hebrews did not attempt to go behind the will of God: what God willed,

[1] Isa. lii. 11 : cf. Dan. xii. 3.
[2] Gen. xviii. 19 ; Ps. i., xviii. 20 f.

that it was their duty to do. But we do, no doubt, get something corresponding to the discussion referred to in the Book of Job, where the sufferer appeals from the God of the traditional kind forced upon him by his friends to a God of a higher morality.

In the case of God the standard of the divine action by which it is adjudged righteous is God's previous action. From the human standpoint the divine righteousness is the self-consistency of the divine conduct; the adherence of His conduct in the present to the standard of His already self-revealed character. The fulness and ethical purity of this idea also may, it is quite manifest, vary greatly. The incomplete abandonment of the national limitation occasionally appears. In the Deutero-Isaiah in particular the three ideas righteousness, deliverance, vengeance, frequently appear side by side; in these cases righteousness is the principle, deliverance the action in which it manifests itself towards Israel, vengeance the action in which it manifests itself towards Israel's foes.

But whatever its limitations, this idea of the divine self-consistency was in itself a valuable one, and owed much to the prophets. Jehovah, exalted by them into the God of the whole world, rules the world not capriciously, but in accordance with His unchanging character. The world and its history is a scene of order, being subject to the guidance of such a God.

Thus, starting with the conception of Jehovah as a national God, whose interests were bound up with those of Israel, and who, in consequence, was pre-eminently a god of war, though also within Israel the patron of justice, we move forward in the Old Testament to the higher conception of Jehovah as God of the whole world, whose interests, therefore, cannot remain mostly those of war, but who more and more becomes the vindicator of justice and righteousness throughout the world. At first, there is often something capricious about Jehovah's anger; it is provoked by involuntary acts of men. And though within the Old Testament this is never entirely outgrown, yet more and more the Divine anger is the manifestation of moral indignation; it grows less and less capricious, and more in harmony with the growing sense of the self-consistency of the Divine action.

II

INDIVIDUAL RESPONSIBILITY—IDEALS OF HUMAN CONDUCT

IN the previous Lecture we have considered some of the leading elements in the Divine character as conceived by the Hebrews, and the influence of these on human conduct. We now approach our subject from the other side, and are directly to consider what the Hebrews counted human excellence. Indirectly this will fill out the picture we have already obtained of the Divine character. For, as we have seen, excellence in human conduct was, from the Hebrew standpoint, what Jehovah approved.

What the Hebrew ideals of conduct were may be gathered from different sources—partly from their laws, which show us what things were definitely prohibited or commanded, partly from the characters which they idealized in their legends or histories, or celebrated in their songs—the patriarchs, for instance, or national leaders such as Moses, David, Josiah; partly from the prophetic censures of the present and visions of the future; partly from the maxims of life which form the proverbial literature of the Old Testament.

Unquestionably the ideals changed with time; there is a marked difference between Moses, as he appears in our early sources, or David, the heroes of the early Hebrews, and Ezra or even Nehemiah, who as man of action may be the better compared with Moses and David, the heroes of post-exilic Judaism. So we may trace changes in the later as compared with the earlier laws, in moral as well as in ritual matters. Unfortunately it would be exceedingly difficult, if not impossible, to use the book of Proverbs for tracing these changes; for though, no doubt, many of the maxims contained in the book are of sufficiently ancient lineage, yet the book in its present form, as well as the various collections contained within it, appears to be of post-exilic origin.

But apart from changes in details, there is one general change of great importance, and to this we must give our main attention. It is the changed estimate of the value of the individual seen in the increased sense of individual responsibility, which marks the later periods; the transition is especially manifest in Jeremiah and Ezekiel.

In ancient times the family or the clan, rather than the individual, formed the unit in society. This lies at the basis of the characteristic institution of primitive societies —the blood-feud. If a man of one clan slay a man of another, the duty lies upon all members of the clan to which the murdered man belongs of exacting a life from the clan of the murderer. It is a matter of comparative indifference whether the life exacted be that of the murderer himself, or that of a fellow-clansman; for it is the clan, not the individual, which is guilty, and it has to purge its guilt by the forfeiture of a life, or an equivalent. It is as a survival of this institution and as an outcome of the feeling of solidarity on which it rested, that we must explain David's action when he handed over to the Gibeonites for execution in expiation of a crime of Saul's seven innocent members of Saul's family.[1] Another effect of this mode of thought which exercised great, if somewhat lessened, influence on the Hebrews long after they had exchanged the nomadic for settled life, was the institution of the ban, or *ḥerem*. The effect of putting the ban into execution was to destroy all who were connected with an individual offender or offenders—the whole of a family, of the population of a city, or of captives in battle. Familiar instances are the destruction of the whole family of Achan, and of the whole of the Amalekite prisoners captured by Saul.[2] Deuteronomy contains a law providing that the ban shall be put into execution in the case of any city in Israel that is seduced into serving other gods: "Thou shalt surely smite the inhabitants with the edge of the sword, banning it, and all that is

[1] 2 Sam. xxi. 1 ff.
[2] Jos. vii. (especially 20-24 f.); 1 Sam. xv. 1-9.

therein, and the cattle thereof, with the edge of the sword."[1]

The ease with which the Hebrews regarded a collection of people as a unity resulted in literary usages which frequently mislead the English reader, and, in particular, cause many of the Psalms to be misunderstood. In their turn these literary usages help us to realize the force and influence of this mode of thought, so alien from our own. It will be worth our while, therefore, to observe a few of the more striking and unmistakable instances.

The general principle of the linguistic usage in question is this : a people, or a clan, or a group of individuals, being conceived as a unity, speak of themselves in the first person *singular*, or are addressed in the second person *singular*. For example : finding that they drove heavily, " Egypt said, Let me flee from the face of Israel ; for Jehovah fighteth for them against Egypt."[2] Israel's reply to the

[1] Deut. xiii. 15.
[2] Exod. xiv. 25. In this and many other cases the English version translates the singulars of the original by plurals, and so conceals the usage from the reader.

Gibeonites affords us another striking instance: "and the men (a collective noun) of Israel said unto the Hivite, Perhaps thou art dwelling in my midst; how, then, should I make a covenant with thee?"[1] Sometimes singulars and plurals interchange, at one time the unity, at another the multiplicity of the people being uppermost in the writer's mind. For instance, in the narrative of Israel's request to pass through Edom, we read: "And Edom said unto him (*i.e.* Israel), Thou shalt not pass through me, lest I come out with the sword against thee. And the children of Israel said unto him, We will go up by the highway; and if we drink of thy water, I and my cattle, then will I give the price of it; let me only, without (doing) anything (else), pass through on my feet. And he said, Thou shalt not pass through."[2]

Connected with this general view of society, with this primitive mode of thought which survived in customs and literary usages long after it had itself become obsolete, is the fact

[1] Jos. ix. 7. [2] Num. xx. 18-20.

that the unit in religion is the people. The two sides to the covenant are Jehovah and Israel; directly the individual as such has no relation to Jehovah, but only in virtue of forming part of Israel. And so the offence of the individual offends Jehovah, because it pollutes that holiness which ought to characterize the people. The audience of the prophets is Israel as a whole; their concern is not primarily with individuals. And the same is frequently true of the laws: "Hear, O Israel, Jehovah our God is one Jehovah; and thou, *i.e.* Israel, shalt love Jehovah thy God with all thine heart, and with all thy soul, and with all thy might."[1] It is due to the fact that it is the people, and the individual only as a member of the people, that has relation with Jehovah that exile from the land of Israel involves cessation of intercourse with Jehovah.[2]

Certain important results for our present subject follow from this ancient view of life. Since the people, or under certain circum-

[1] Deut. vi. 5.   [2] *Cf.* p. 45 above.

stances a smaller group such as the clan or the family, is the social and religious unit, it follows that the full force of the religious sanction is only felt in the case of what we may term the national morality. Israel as a whole is to be holy because Jehovah is holy. Indirectly this unquestionably affected the individual; so much so, indeed, that the unholiness of an individual polluted the nation. But it is to the nation as a whole rather than to the individual offender himself that Jehovah manifests His displeasure at the unholiness produced by the fault of an individual. Achan, an individual, violates the command of Jehovah not to take of the devoted stuff of the Canaanites, but it is not himself merely that sins; Israel, as a whole, is, by his error, rendered guilty.[1] Achan alone took of the 'devoted stuff,' but it is thus that Jehovah addresses Joshua: "Get thee up; wherefore art thou thus fallen upon thy face? Israel hath sinned; yea, they have even transgressed my covenant, which I commanded them; yea,

[1] Jos. vii. 11.

they have even taken of the devoted thing; and have also stolen, and dissembled also, and they have even put it among their own stuff." And because through the offence of an individual Israel as a whole has sinned, Israel as a whole is also punished by ill-success in battle; and it is only through this national disaster that attention is drawn to the offending member.[1]

In the same way Jehovah manifests His anger at the entirely unintentional offence of Jonathan by refusing to give Saul an answer and so troubling the whole people.[2] An unexpiated crime renders the whole community guilty before Jehovah;[3] and, as a consequence, in Deuteronomy Israel is frequently exhorted to punish crime, and so "to exterminate the evil" from its midst.[4]

But where the morality of the individual is thus so closely bound up with that of the people as a whole, it almost necessarily follows that morality will be externally regarded.

[1] Jos. vii. 12 ff.   [2] 1 Sam. xiv. 37 ff.
[3] See, *e.g.*, Deut. xxi. 1-9.
[4] Deut. xiii. 5, xvii. 7, xix. 19, xxi. 21, xxii. 21-24, xxiv. 7.

Morality is a matter of outward act, not of inward disposition. For the deeper conception of morality a clear perception of individual responsibility is requisite.

Now the growth of this sense of individual responsibility is to be traced within the Old Testament. In importance it ranks with the transition from the national to the universal conception of God, and the consequent widening of the range of moral obligation. In the one case the moral sense is enlarged, in the other it is deepened and intensified. Through the one change the Israelite came to feel his obligation to all men irrespective of race; through the other his immediate and direct responsibility to God. Neither the one change nor the other exercised at large its full effect; the influence of old and discarded doctrines lingered long; but in both cases the new principles were at work.

Some signs of the breaking down of the old conception of the indifference of the individual may be already traced in the older stories. We recall Abraham's question relative to Sodom—" Wilt thou destroy the righteous with the wicked ? "[1] or David's plea, " Lo, I have sinned and I have done perversely; but these sheep, what have they done? let thine hand, I pray thee, be against me, and against my father's house."[2] The last case is of double interest. The prayer is that the effect of David's individual sin may be limited, yet not to himself only, but to his father's house.

In Deuteronomy we have a law which would read strangely indeed except in the light of the prevalence of ideas to which I have been drawing attention. This law directly forbids a practice which quite naturally sprang out of the conception that the family, not the individual, is the social unit. The law runs : " The fathers shall not be put to death for the children, neither shall the children be put to death for the fathers; every man shall be put to death for his own sin."[3]

[1] Gen. xviii. 23. [2] 2 Sam. xxiv. 17.
[3] Deut. xxiv. 16 ; cf. 2 Kings xiv. 6.

But we can see the change most clearly in the teaching of the prophets Jeremiah and Ezekiel, and it is by no means accidental that they both lived at the time when the Hebrew national life was closed by the Babylonian conquest and the exile of the greater and most influential part of the nation to Babylon.

In Ezekiel we see all the force of extreme reaction, and a consequently very exaggerated counter-doctrine. Individualism has never been more baldly stated. The prophet challenges the popular proverb: "The fathers have eaten sour grapes, and the children's teeth are set on edge,"[1] *i.e.* the children suffer for the father's sins. This proverb the exiles were constantly throwing in the teeth of the prophet as he tried to move them to penitence. We, they said, are innocent; our sufferings in exile are the punishment for our fathers' sins. In reply the prophet asserts that in future at any rate this proverb will be untrue: each individual shall suffer for his own sin. In this, of course, the prophet is

[1] Ezek. xviii. 2.

false to the facts of life; suffering is not proportioned to the sin of the individual. It is this false view of the meaning of suffering, to which we shall return in our last discussion, that vitiates to so large an extent Ezekiel's doctrine of the individual. But the ground on which he bases it is sound as it was novel. These are the words in which he states it, speaking in the name of Jehovah: "Behold, all souls are mine: as the soul of the father, so also the soul of the son is mine;"[1] that is to say, the individual in himself and independently belongs to Jehovah; the relationship is not, as in the old doctrine, mediate and based on the individual's relation to the nation, but direct and immediate. It will be observed, then, that Ezekiel brings out the value, independence, and direct responsibility of the individual in connection with the question of sin and punishment. We shall see that Jeremiah regards these moral factors from a very different standpoint. But before leaving Ezekiel, let us take account of a very

[1] Ezek. xviii. 4.

instructive instance of the limited extent to which a new doctrine affects even the person who promulgates it. Ezekiel, the author of as sharp and unqualified an individualism as it is possible to conceive, nevertheless gathers together in his allegory in chap. xvi. all the sins, as it were, of past generations, and charges them upon the Israel of his day. Israel of all time is thus regarded as a moral unity.

Jeremiah, the earlier contemporary of Ezekiel, never so clearly enunciates a doctrine of individual responsibility; but he is far more influential in securing a sense of the religious and moral value of the individual. He, too, was led to this new position by the fact of exile; and what he teaches is that the relation which had been thought to exist between Jehovah and Israel might exist between Jehovah and the individual. It is no mere question with him of retribution. While of old the relation had been between Jehovah and the nation, Jehovah had nevertheless made known His will to the nation through certain individuals—prophets or priests or national leaders. Faced by the certain approach of exile and the destruction of the national life, Jeremiah rose to the conviction that what in the past had been the privilege of special individuals—direct intercourse with God— might be the privilege of all. In the case of every man, the law of Jehovah might be written on the heart; that is to say, the Divine voice might speak within him as it had spoken to the prophet.[1] Exile might come; the nation might perish; but with it Jehovah would not perish; rather out of the disaster would come a higher privilege for those individuals who would claim it—direct participation in Jehovah, instead of a merely intermediate relation to him through the national life.

What Jeremiah perceived beforehand, the exile necessarily enforced practically. According to the conception prevalent in David's time, the exiles could not have worshipped Jehovah.[2] As a matter of fact, they did; and

[1] Jer. xxxi. 23 f.   [2] See above, p. 45.

in so doing, realized that, as sacrifice and burnt-offering which could not be offered in exile were unnecessary to religion,[1] so also residence in the land of Jehovah or the existence of the nation were unnecessary, but that the individual, wherever he was, was the true religious unit, and, as such, capable of intercourse with God. With the return from exile, sacrifice was resumed, and something of a national life revived; but the individualism which Jeremiah had taught and the exile must have fostered, though it may have been in some way retarded by the change, and did not become universally prevalent, survived as a new element in religious life, and as a new and potent factor in morality.

To the combined effect of the two great changes which we have now observed—the transcendence of the national conception of God and the development of a sense of the moral and religious value of the individual —we may trace a new type or ideal of life which comes before us in the post-exilic

[1] Psalms li. 16; xl. 6 ff.

period—that of the humble man. In early times men trembled at the manifestation of Jehovah's anger.[1] But there is a fear that is not craven, and is not inspired by a purely unmoral exhibition of power; there is a sense of the immeasurable moral difference between the individual man and his Maker—man in his sin and imperfection, God in His purity and might. Now this sense, this feeling which we term 'humility,' first becomes prominent after the exile, and is surely due on the one hand to the greater and nobler idea of God, and on the other to the new conviction that it is individual men who have intercourse with Him. The ideal is thus described in perhaps its most classic setting : " I dwell in the high and holy place, with him also that is of a contrite and humble spirit, to revive the spirit of the humble, and to revive the heart of the contrite ones. For I will not contend for ever, neither will I be always wroth : for the spirit should fail before me, and the souls, *i.e.* the individuals, which I have made."[2] Or again, in

[1] See, *e.g.*, 1 Sam. vi. 20.   [2] Isa. lvii. 15 f.—a post-exilic passage.

another late piece of literature: "the sacrifices of God are a broken spirit; a broken and a contrite heart, O God, thou wilt not despise."[1] This praise of the crushed in spirit is unknown to the early literature. In another form we find this ideal of humility in the eighth Psalm, which brings together the frailty, and yet the greatness of man, in consequence of God's visitation of him; or again, in admissions of Job.

This is one of the most striking among the new virtues or moral ideals that were created during the course of Israel's history. It will only be possible in the very briefest way to refer to some of the more general aspects of Hebrew ideals of life.

In the light of what has been said as to the nation or family rather than the individual being the social unit, it is not surprising to find the value attached to public spirit, to devotion to the common cause. It is praise of public spirit and condemnation of the lack of it that characterizes the earliest

[1] Psalm li. 17.

extant piece of Hebrew literature—the Song of Deborah :—

> " For that the leaders took the lead in Israel,
> For that the people offered themselves willingly ;
> Bless ye Jehovah." [1]

These opening words form the keynote of the song. The tribes that participate in the battle are honourably mentioned ; those that kept to their own concerns are reproached ; and—most significant of all—Jael's public spirit more than covers her treacherous murder of Sisera, which must otherwise have offended the moral feeling even of her age ; for Sisera was her guest, and the guest, whether foreigner or fellow-tribesman, had the right of protection and safety.

Again, the famous characters of early Israel are the national leaders—Moses, who created the nation ; the judges, who recovered the people from subjection to their enemies ; Saul and David, who created the monarchy, and so consolidated the national unity and power.

Perhaps, beyond any other, David presents

[1] Judges v. 2.

in actual life the early Hebrew ideal of excellence; his magnanimity towards Saul, his love for Jonathan, the success he achieved for his people, and other kindred virtues, made him renowned in song and story. Elements in his character and practice which offend us—his sensuality, his cruelty to his foes—did not offend his contemporaries. But the history of David not only affords a concrete instance of Hebrew ideals of conduct: it also brings strikingly to light the moral sensitiveness of the people. For simple beauty, for moral earnestness, the story of Nathan's rebuke of David's sin,[1] which was probably written within a generation or two of the event, stands unsurpassed in the moral literature of the world. The moral standard of the age of David was not our standard; it approved things that the moral sense of our time condemns; the range of moral obligation was limited. But the moral spirit of the people was quick and sensitive; and when their moral standard

[1] 2 Sam. xii.

was violated, they did not shrink from condemning it even in their most popular hero.

If we glance at the early laws, we again see the noble elements which already characterize early Hebrew morality. Some injustice is done to that morality by the undue stress laid on the Ten Commandments and the constant recital of them. Hebrew morality, much less Christian morality, is far from even being summarized in these. One limitation, however, which extends beyond these, and was characteristic of Hebrew morality, may be noticed in passing : the Ten Commandments forbid false witness—*i.e.*, forbid lying to the manifest hurt of another ; but they do not forbid lying as such. Truthfulness in the abstract is not a virtue that is much appraised in the Old Testament, particularly in its earlier parts ; and indeed the Hebrew language has no very specific and distinctive term to express the idea. The word generally translated 'Truth' means originally and very frequently in usage, simply steadfastness or faithfulness.

Far more illustrative of the character of Hebrew morality than the Ten Commandments are such laws as these which I will cite from the earliest Code (eighth century B.C.): "Ye shall not afflict any widow or fatherless child. If thou afflict them in any wise, and they cry at all unto me, I will surely hear their cry: and my wrath shall wax hot, and I will kill you with the sword."[1] "If thou lend money to any of my people with thee that is poor, thou shalt not be to him as a creditor: neither shalt thou take interest of him. If thou at all take thy neighbour's garment in pledge, thou shalt restore it unto him by the time that the sun goes down; for that is his only covering, it is his garment for his skin; wherein shall he sleep"—viz., if you keep it over-night?[2] "If thou meet thine enemy's ox or his ass going astray, thou shalt surely bring it back to him again."[3] "Thou shalt not (unduly) favour a poor man in his

[1] Exod. xxii. 22 f.　　[2] Exod. xxii. 25–27.
[3] Exod. xxiii. 4.

cause."[1] These laws may illustrate the humanity and high-mindedness of the early Hebrews in their dealings between man and man.[2] The conduct which is here implied was, it will be remembered, only exacted or expected within the limits of the Hebrew nation. But within this limitation, it was not in some respects easy of being improved. The same warm humanity, and especially the same tender regard for the weak and helpless, breathes through the Deuteronomic legislation, which has been so well characterized by Dr Driver. "*Humanity* is the author's ruling motive, wherever considerations of religion or morality do not force him to repress it. Accordingly, great emphasis is laid upon the exercise of

[1] Exod. xxiii. 3.
[2] Certain laws sometimes cited as illustrating the humanity of the Hebrews are, however, not true instances. One of these is the law of Exod. xxiii. 19 (=Deut. xiv. 21), which is cited (*e.g.*, by Mr Lecky in his *History of European Morals*, ii. p. 162, n. 4, Cabinet Edition) in proof of the kindness of the Hebrews to animals. But the prohibition is in all probability based on the superstitious rather than on the cruel character of the act. Deut. xxii. 6 f. is, perhaps, another case in point. On both passages, see Dr Driver's *Commentary*.

philanthropy, promptitude, and liberality towards those in difficulty or want, as the indigent in need of a loan (xv. 7–11; xxiii. 20 (19 f.), a slave at the time of his manumission (xv. 13–15), a neighbour who has lost any of his property (xxii. 1–4), a poor man obliged to borrow on pledge (xxiv. 6, 12 f.), a fugitive slave (xxiv. 7), a hired servant (xxiv. 14 f.), and in the law for the disposition of the triennial tithe (xiv. 21 f.): the landless Levite (xii. 12, 18 f.; xiv. 27, 29; xvi. 11, 14; xxvi. 11, 12 f.); and 'the stranger'—*i.e.*, the unprotected foreigner settled in Israel—'the fatherless and the widow,' are repeatedly commended to the Israelite's charity or regard (xiv. 29 . . .), especially at the time of the great annual pilgrimages (xii. 12, 11; xiv. 27; xvi. 11, 14; xxvi. 11), when he and his household partook together before God of the bounty of the soil, and might the more readily respond to an appeal for benevolence. Gratitude, and a sense of sympathy, evoked by the recollection of Israel's own past, are frequently appealed to as the motives by which the Israelite should in such cases be actuated (x. 19; ... xv. 15; xvi. 12 ...). A spirit of forbearance, equity, and regard for the feelings of others underlies the regulations of v. 14b.; xx. 5–9; xx. 10 ff. ... Several of these provisions are prompted in particular by the endeavour to ameliorate the condition of dependents, and to mitigate the cruelties of war. Not, indeed, that similar considerations are absent from the older legislation, ... but they are developed in Deuteronomy with an emphasis and distinctness which give a character to the entire work. The author speaks out of a warm heart himself; and he strives to kindle a warm response in the heart of every one whom he addresses. Nowhere else in the Old Testament do we breathe such an atmosphere of generous devotion to God, and of large-hearted benevolence towards man; nowhere else are duties and motives set forth with greater depth and tenderness of feeling, or with more winning and persuasive eloquence; and nowhere else is it shown with the same fulness of detail how high and noble principles may be applied so as to elevate and refine the entire life of the community."[1]

The considerations of religion or morality to which the author just quoted refers, as limiting the humanity of Deuteronomy, remind us of certain marked differences between our own and the Deuteronomic standpoint. Any such thing as religious toleration was, of course, unknown to the Hebrews.

The spirit which characterizes the two codes already referred to, still governs the earliest section of the Priestly Code—the so-called Law of Holiness, which appears to have been compiled in the early part of the sixth century B.C. It is succinctly expressed in the saying of which the Old Testament origin is sometimes forgotten: "Thou shalt love thy neighbour as thyself."[2]

Certainly in the last great body of law—

[1] Driver, *Critical and Exegetical Commentary on Deuteronomy*, pp. xxiv. f.

[2] Lev. xix. 18; and compare in detail, *e.g.*, Lev. xxv. 25, 35–39. For the limited application of the saying, see p. 47.

—the main part of the Priestly Code—this spirit is less manifest. But the chief subject of that law was ritual rather than political and social. This needs to be borne in mind.[1] Further, if we would judge the spirit of the age out of which it springs, and in which it was influential, we must also take account of other characteristic products of the age, such as the Book of Proverbs, and at least many of the Psalms.

But although the discussion, even in brief, of the moral ideals of post-exilic Judaism is, on the present occasion, precluded by the limit of these Lectures, it must not be supposed that the details of Hebrew morality become less worthy just when, as our previous discussions have shown us, the people were learning that moral obligation was not limited to men of one's own race, and that the individual was directly and immediately responsible to God for his life and conduct. There is one passage in the post-exilic literature which by itself may suffice to prevent so false

[1] See above, p. 63.

a conclusion. It has not unfitly been said that if we want a summary of moral duties from the Old Testament, it might better be found in Job's soliloquy as he turns away from his friends and reviews his past life, than in the Ten Commandments. Let me conclude this brief summary of Hebrew ideals of life by quoting part of this speech. With the book of which it forms a part, it can hardly have been written before the fifth century B.C., and it may have been written a century or two later. The speech is mainly a repudiation of certain crimes or neglected duties. It is easy to gather from it what was the author's positive ideal of life.

> "If I have walked with vanity,
> And my foot hath hasted to deceit.
>
> . . . . .
>
> If my step hath turned out of my way,
> And mine heart walked after mine eyes,
> And if any spot hath cleaved to my hands;
> Then let me sow, and another eat;
> Yea, let the produce of my field be rooted out.
>
> . . . . .
>
> If I did despise the cause of my man-servant, or of my maid-servant,
> When they contended with me;

What, then, shall I do when God riseth up?
And when He visiteth, what shall I answer Him!
Did not He that made me in the womb make him?
And did not one fashion us in the womb?
If I have withheld the poor from (their) desire,
Or have caused the eyes of the widow to fail;
Or have eaten my morsel alone,
And the fatherless hath not eaten thereof;
(Nay, from my youth he grew up with me as with a father,
And I have been her guide from my mother's womb,)
If I have seen any perish for want of clothing,
Or that the needy had no covering;
If his loins have not blessed me,
And if he were not warmed with the fleece of my sheep;
If I have lifted up my hand against the fatherless,
Because I saw my help in the gate;
Then let my shoulder fall from the shoulder blade,
And mine arm be broken from the bone.

  . . . . .

If I have made gold my hope,
And have said to the fine gold (thou art) my confidence;
If I rejoiced because my wealth was great,
And because mine hand had gotten much;

  . . . . .

If I have rejoiced at the destruction of him that hated me,
Or lifted up myself when evil found him;
(Yea, I suffered not my mouth to sin,
By asking his life with a·curse;)

  . . . . .

If . . . I covered my transgression,

By hiding mine iniquity in my bosom;
Because I feared the great multitude,
And the contempt of families terrified me,
So that I kept silence and went out at the door.

. . . . .

If my land cry out against me,
And the furrows thereof weep together;
If I have eaten the fruits thereof without money,
Or have caused the owners thereof to lose their life;
Let thistles grow instead of wheat,
And cockle instead of barley."[1]

[1] Job xxxi. 5 ff.

III

THE MOTIVE OF CONDUCT

WE have now seen, to some extent, what ideals of conduct prevailed among the Hebrews, what were the virtues they approved and the vices they condemned, and within what limitations they felt bound to exercise these virtues. Another important question arises in considering the morality—actual and theoretical—of any people, though it can only be satisfactorily answered when the people under consideration have left behind them a literature of reflection. The question I refer to is this—Why did the people or the individual pursue the conduct that commanded their moral approbation? What was their motive in doing right? Why were they prepared to do what they thought right at the cost of present inconvenience and suffering? Why, to take a concrete instance from one of the Psalmists, when a man swore, as he subsequently discovered, to his own hurt, did he not repudiate his oath?[1]

This, it will be at once recognized, is one of the fundamental questions in speculative ethics, and closely allied to the still more fundamental question—What is right? What is the ultimate difference between right and wrong? This most fundamental of all ethical questions is never directly raised in this form in the Old Testament. So far as the attitude of the Hebrews towards it can be discovered, they tacitly held that whatever was the will of Jehovah was right. Certainly they were not in this respect deliberate utilitarians; they did not define right as that which produces pleasure, wrong as that which produces pain. On the other hand, they did not, as we have already observed, go behind the will of Jehovah; they had no clear conception of a moral law independent of that will.

But when we turn from the question of what is right to the motive with which what

[1] Ps. xv. 4.

was held to be right was done, we certainly find it emerging in the Old Testament. Indirectly it is answered again and again in the law, in the prophets, in the proverbial literature; directly it is raised and tentatively answered in the book of Job—the most striking instance in Biblical literature of the actual discussion of a moral problem.

There can be no question that the motive which is predominant in Hebrew literature is thoroughly utilitarian. The people as a whole and the individual are alike exhorted to do what is right on the ground that it is advantageous so to do. Let us illustrate this. The great objects of a Hebrew's desire—and not alone of his—were wealth and long life. Personified wisdom is commended to men on the ground that "length of days is in her right hand; in her left hand are riches and honour"—that is to say, she can bestow these things on those that love her.[1] Solomon is commended because, when he had the opportunity of obtaining whatever he wanted,

[1] Prov. iii. 16.

he did not ask for either long life or riches.[1] Remember this, and then recall the commandment with its motive — Honour thy father and thy mother: that thy days may be long upon the land which Jehovah thy God giveth thee.[2] Or this exhortation of Isaiah's: If ye be willing and obedient (*i.e.* to the word and will of Jehovah), ye shall eat the good of the land; but if ye refuse and rebel, ye shall be devoured with the sword.[3] Or of Amos: Seek good and not evil, that ye may live.[4]

The passages which I have just cited—the one from a law-giver, the other two from the prophets—are not isolated and exceptional instances; they are thoroughly characteristic expressions of the motives which both the law and the prophets constantly suggest.

Deuteronomy is a law addressed to Israel as a whole; it exhorts the people to obey Jehovah's commandments, promising that obedience will ensure the long continuance and

---

[1] 1 Kings iii. 11.   [2] Exod. xx. 12.
[3] Isa. i. 19.   [4] Amos v. 14.

THE MOTIVE OF CONDUCT

prosperity of the nation, disobedience its immediate destruction. Sayings such as the following occur again and again : " Observe and hear all these words which I command thee, that it may go well with thee, and with thy children after thee for ever, when thou doest that which is good and right in the eyes of Jehovah thy God."[1] "Ye shall walk in all the way which Jehovah your God hath commanded you, that ye may live, and that it may be well with you, and that ye may prolong your days in the land which ye shall possess."[2] "Behold I set before you this day a blessing and a curse : the blessing if ye shall hearken unto the commandments of Jehovah your God ; and the curse, if ye shall not hearken unto the commandments of Jehovah your God."[3]

A similar motive is eloquently set forth in the concluding homily to the Law of Holiness, which opens with these promises of Jehovah : " If you follow my statutes, and keep my

---

[1] Deut. xii. 28 ; cf. iv. 40, v. 29, vi. 18, xxii. 7.
[2] v. 33 ; cf. iv. 40, xi. 9, xxx. 18-20.   [3] xi. 27 f.

commandments, and do them, then I will give you your rains in their seasons, and the land shall yield its increase, and the trees of the field shall yield their fruit. And your threshing shall last to the vintage, and the vintage shall last to the sowing time; and you shall eat your bread to the full, and dwell in your land securely. And I will give you peace in the land, and you shall lie down, and none shall make you afraid. I will cause wild beasts to disappear out of the land, and the sword shall not go through your land. And you shall chase your enemies, and they shall fall before your sword. . . . And I will look with favour upon you, and make you fruitful and multiply you; and I will fulfil my covenant with you. And you shall eat old stores long kept, and you shall take out the old to make room for the new."[1] Subsequently a long series of the misfortunes which are to befall the people in case they are disobedient is recounted.

[1] Lev. xxvi. 2-10 (Driver and White's translation in the "Polychrome" Bible).

And when we turn to that great Hebrew compendium of individual morality, the book of Proverbs, we find the same motive constantly brought forward, " Honour Jehovah with thy substance, and with the firstfruits of all thine increase. So shall thy barns be filled with plenty, and thy fats shall overflow with new wine." [1] " The fear of Jehovah prolongeth days, but the years of the wicked shall be shortened." [2] " There shall no mischief happen to the righteous ; but the wicked shall be filled with evil." [3] But it is unnecessary to multiply instances ; the same motive is implicit in every part of the book.

The same note appears in many of the Psalms ; for example : " What man is he that desireth life, and loveth many days, that he may see good ? Keep thy tongue from evil, and thy lips from speaking guile. Depart from evil and do good ; seek peace and pursue it." [4] " Wait on the Lord, and keep

[1] Prov. iii. 9 f.   [2] x. 27.
[3] xii. 21.   [4] Ps. xxxiv. 12-14.

His way, and He shall exalt thee to inherit the land." [1]

We shall have to observe immediately the awakening of the Hebrew consciousness to a higher motive of conduct. But that awakening took place in individuals rather than in the mass of the people. And side by side with the lofty motives that appear in the book of Job, and in some of the Psalms, we find in literature at least as late, if not later, the old utilitarian motive still dominant. The books of Chronicles are among the latest books of the Old Testament: they were obviously not compiled much before 300 B.C. But they are peculiarly distinguished by a fondness for representing "a great calamity or deliverance as the punishment of wickedness or the reward of virtue." [2]

Now, to infer from these characteristics of the legal, prophetic, and moral writings of the Hebrews that their morality, the morality of

[1] Ps. xxxvii. 34.
[2] Driver, *Introduction to the Literature of the Old Testament* (sixth edition), p. 526, where proof and illustrations of the statement may be found.

the people as a whole, and of all the individuals among them, was a mere calculation of what course of life would give them the greatest length of days and the largest amount of material prosperity, would be illegitimate and unfair—illegitimate partly because we can see in actual life that many men have other than the utilitarian motives of the maxims they profess, and partly because a further examination of the same literature that we have been considering indicates the presence of other motives.

This latter fact is especially true of Deuteronomy, which, in its turn, for this side of its teaching, is dependent on the prophets, and, above all, on Hosea.

"The love of God, an all-absorbing sense of personal devotion to Him, is propounded in Deuteronomy as the primary spring of human action (vi. 5); it is the duty which is the direct corollary of the character of God, and of Israel's relation to Him; the Israelite is to love Him with undivided affection, to 'cleave' to Him (x. 20; xi. 22; xiii. 5;

xxx. 20), to renounce everything that is in any degree inconsistent with loyalty to Him." [1]

This is a thoroughly just appreciation of the great law-book, and enables us to see that there was room, at any rate in the religion of the seventh century, for a far nobler motive to conduct than that of a careful calculating self-interest. At the same time, the presence of the motive previously discussed is a very important fact, and not to be neglected. The truth is, we have side by side two motives—a higher and a lower; whether the higher was clearly primary in the mind of the authors we cannot say, but it is only too probable that the lower motive was the more largely effective. It needed an actual test clearly to distinguish between them; to determine how far the "love of God" could secure the doing of His will when it not merely failed to bring any striking material prosperity, but, on the contrary, entailed material loss and suffering.

[1] Driver, *Deuteronomy*, p. xxi.; *cf.* pp. xxxi, f.

THE MOTIVE OF CONDUCT

In the case of the nation, this test was afforded by the exile; in the case of the individual, the test was often enough present, but only became clearly perceptible after the sense of individual responsibility had become highly developed; and the old belief, based on the theory of solidarity,[1] that a man was justly punished in his descendants,[2] had been discarded.[3] Consequently, the meaning of disaster and suffering alike in the case of the people and the individual only gained any considerable attention in and after the exile. It is the Deutero-Isaiah who gains a new and higher standpoint with regard to the national disaster; it is the author of the book of Job who refuted the prevalent theory of suffering, and in so doing weakened the hold of the utilitarian motive of conduct on the individual, and thus made way for a nobler motive.

I can merely refer in the briefest way possible to the Deutero-Isaiah's position,

---
[1] See above, pp. 77–90.
[2] *Cf.*, *e.g.*, Job xxi. 19.
[3] Deut. vii. 10; Ezek. xviii.

simply stating the view that seems to me the correct one of the crucial passages without attempting to defend it in detail.

In the opening words of his prophecy the great exilic prophet announces that Jehovah's people have received double for all their sins [1] —*i.e.*, that all their suffering has not been penal. In the course of the prophecy, the people comes before us personified as the servant of Jehovah.[2] We find that this servant has entrusted to him the charge of enlightening and instructing the Gentiles,[3] and that to carry out his task, the servant had " to give his back to the smiters and his cheeks to those that plucked out the beard." [4] Ultimately Jehovah exalts His much-despised servant Israel, and the nations confess that it was for their transgressions that Israel had suffered, and that through the stripes which had fallen on Israel they had obtained healing.[5]

Here, then, we find a new national ideal; it is no longer with this writer material pro-

[1] Isa. xl. 2.
[2] So quite obviously in xli. 8; xliv. 1, 2, 21. xlii. 1-4; xlix. 6.   [4] l. 6.   [5] Isa. lii. 13-liii. 12.

sperity in the land which Jehovah has given to Israel; it is co-operation with Jehovah, even at the cost of national disaster and suffering, in the work of enlightening the world.

We turn to the question of individual suffering and its relation to the motive of the conduct of the individual.

The Satan immediately raises the question of motive in the prologue to the book of Job. "Doth Job fear God for nought?"[1] God may be right in claiming that Job is perfect, but—so the Satan insinuates—that, after all, only means that Job knows how to get the best of things. His piety pays him. God's method of governing man leaves no room for disinterested piety—no room, at least, for really putting it to the test. Job lives a good life, because it makes him rich in cattle. It is unnecessary to repeat the familiar story; we know how the test comes. Job is stripped of all his wealth, smitten with disease, and on the point of death. Piety no longer pays materially: can it stand the test?

[1] Job i. 9.

The speeches of the friends illustrate the prevalent doctrine that the motive of good conduct is the material prosperity that it brings and the length of days that it secures. In the case of Eliphaz we seem to detect that double motive that marks the book of Deuteronomy; he, in his last speech, shows some feeling that the possession of Jehovah, harmony with His will, is the highest reward of a righteous life. "If thou return to the Almighty, thou shalt be built up; if thou put away unrighteousness far from thy tents. And lay thou thy treasure in the dust, and the (gold of) Ophir among the stones of the brooks, and the Almighty shall be thy treasure and precious silver unto thee. For then thou shalt delight thyself in the Almighty, and shalt lift up thy face unto God."[1] But even this fine passage is also marked by the presence of the lower doctrine, that it is well to be righteous because it ensures material prosperity, that man gets a good return for his service of God.

It is in the attitude of Job himself that we

[1] Job xxii. 23-26.

see the new motive coming to light in its
purity. It is important to bear in mind that
the author of the book held no doctrine of
reward in a future life. He is faced terribly
and simply enough with this question—Has
he been wise in his mode of his life? He
has been righteous, but his righteousness has
met with the reward of dire misfortunes. In
consequence, every one, even of his friends,
considers that he must have sinned greatly,
and this is the final and greatest aggravation
of his sufferings. Why, then, has he been
righteous? Why should he still "hold fast
to his integrity"? And the answer the book
gives to this question is, that he has not been
unwise; that his motive in being righteous
had not been the wealth which his good life
had at first brought him; and, therefore, that
he cannot and will not follow the request of
his friends to be unrighteous, and admit sins
which he had never committed in the hope of
an alleviation of his sufferings. In spite of
all, he holds fast to his integrity, and rises
to the belief that, if not in this life, yet here-

after, God will vindicate his character. He appeals, as I have said in a previous Lecture, from the traditional God whom he knows now to be unreal to a truly moral God; and in communion with Him he finds more than compensation for all his sufferings. This is his true wealth, that whereas a godless man cannot come before God, he is confident that he will do so.[1]

Briefly expressed in modern terms, the answer of the book to the Satan's question —Does Job fear God for nought? *i.e.*, do not men do what is right because it pays them best? is this—Job does not fear God for nought; but the return which he gets, as he sees when put to the test, is not wealth, and comfort, and esteem of men, but the possibility that comes by it of living in God's presence and enjoying His society. He loves and serves God for God's own sake, and not for any of the accidental outward advantages of a good life.

The same problem is raised, and a similar

[1] Job xiii. 16.

answer given, in some psalms written by men of kindred spirit with the author of Job. For instance, the author of the 73rd Psalm was at first distressed at the contrast between the wicked who enjoy all manner of prosperity, who have no torments, whose body is sound and plump, who partake not of the travail of mortals, nor are plagued like other men,[1] and his own distress, plagued as he was all the day, rebuked every morning. And in his mind, too, there arose the question—Had he been wise in being righteous? At first he was inclined to say, "Surely in vain have I cleansed my heart, and washed my hands in innocency"[2]; but his final answer is, that the possession of God outweighs all his troubles.

> Whom have I (to care for) in heaven?
> And possessing thee I have pleasure in nothing upon earth.
> Though my flesh and my heart should have wasted away,
> God would for ever be the rock of my heart and my portion.

[1] Ps. lxxiii. 4 f.   [2] ver. 13.

> For behold, they that go afar from thee shall perish;
> Everyone that wantonly deserts thee, dost thou clean put out.
> But as for me, to be near to God is my happiness;
> I have put my trust in the Lord Jehovah.
> That I may rehearse all thy works.[1]

Somewhat later we find in a remarkable saying attributed in the Mishna to Antigonus of Soko, who lived in the second century B.C., a direct exhortation to the disinterested service of God. This noble-minded Jewish teacher used to say, "Be not as slaves that minister to the lord with a view to receive recompense; but be as slaves that minister to the lord without a view to receive recompense."[2]

It is no small matter that, quite apart from a doctrine of a future life, which may, and often does, tend to the confusion of motives, the quasi-utilitarian motive which runs through so much of the Old Testament is thus clearly and deliberately discarded by some of the latest of the sacred writers; that alike the Hebrew nation and the Hebrew individual were taught

[1] Ps. lxxiii. 25-28. The translation is from Cheyne, *The Book of Psalms*.
[2] *Pirkê Abhôth*, i. 3.

by them that conduct had a higher aim than the outward prosperity which it might bring, to wit, co-operation with God in action, communion with Him in spirit. The change has been noted by Lord Bacon, who is sometimes a keen-sighted interpreter of Scripture. " Prosperity is the blessing of the Old Testament; Adversity is the blessing of the New; which carrieth the greater benediction, and the clearer revelation of God's favour. Yet even in the Old Testament, if you listen to David's harp, you shall hear as many hearse-like airs as carols; and the pencil of the Holy Ghost hath laboured more in describing the afflictions of Job than the felicities of Solomon."[1]

New ideas obtain their full effect but slowly; the old ideas which they in part replace, in part remain effective; and in part it is in some cases well that they do, for the new idea is not the whole truth. Of these general laws of the growth of ideas, the three main changes which we have discussed in these

[1] Essay on *Adversity*.

Lectures furnish illustrations. It was long after Amos before the great mass, even of the Jews, realized that Jehovah was God of the whole world, and that in consequence moral obligation extended to all men, and not only to one's fellow-countrymen. Indeed, the old doctrine, at least in the form that one's obligations are largely confined to those of the same religion, is not even yet fully outgrown. In the case of the second change, by which a due sense of individual responsibility was developed, we have an illustration of abiding elements of truth in the old doctrine. Ezekiel, as we saw, in enunciating his bald individualistic doctrine, was blind to facts of life—stern, yet indisputable facts—which remind us that the individual life is no isolated thing. In the New Testament both ideas gain due recognition, and are harmonized— there we find the strongest insistence on individual responsibility; but there we find also the idea and ideal of a common life of the whole—the kingdom of God is a unity, the ideal is the single body of Christ of which all are members. And the motive of conduct—how slowly, how inadequately, does motive become purified ; how long the old doctrine of the direct and proportionate suffering for sin lingers with its almost necessary corollary, that we should do right in order that we may prosper and have comfort. But, again, the Old Testament culminates in the New ; and low and impure motives for good outward conduct give way, where the truly Christian spirit enters, to that which makes the inward character and the outward action a pure and noble harmony—" the constraining love of Christ."

APPENDIX

I HAVE referred in the foregoing pages more than once to the similarity between the thought of the Moabites with regard to their god Chemosh and that of the early Hebrews with regard to Jehovah. No one who reads the inscription of Mesha (who lived in the ninth century B.C.) can fail to observe this. It has been very frequently reproduced, but, for the convenience of the reader, I give here a translation of the first part of it. The latter part contains little reference to Chemosh. My translation is based on that of Dr Driver (*Notes on the Hebrew Text of the Books of Samuel*, p. lxxxvii, f.), but I have changed the order of the words in accordance with the demands of English idiom, and I have omitted marks of interrogation and the like. The uncertainties as to the decipherment or meanings of a few words thus indicated do not affect the general tenour of the inscription with which alone it is my present object to enable the reader to acquaint himself. For all details he should refer to the commentary accompanying Dr Driver's text and translation.

"I am Mesha, son of Chemoshmelek, King of Moab, the Daibonite. My father reigned over Moab for thirty years, and I reigned after my father. And I made this high place for Chemosh in QRHH, a high place of salvation, because he had saved me from all the kings, and because he had let me see my pleasure on all them that hated me. Omri was king over Israel, and he afflicted Moab for many days, because Chemosh was angry with his land. And his son succeeded him; and he also said, I will afflict Moab. In my days said he thus; but I saw my pleasure on him, and on his house, and Israel perished with an everlasting destruction. And Omri took possession of the land of Měhēdeba, and it (*i.e.* Israel) dwelt therein during his days, and half his son's days, forty years; but Chemosh restored it in my days. And I built Ba'al-Maon, and I made in it the reservoir; and I built Qiryathên. And the men of Gad had dwelt in the land of 'Ataroth from of old; and the king of Israel had built for himself 'Ataroth. And I fought against the city and took it. And I slew all the people of the city, a gazing-stock unto Chemosh, and unto Moab. And I brought back thence the altar-hearth of Davdoh, and I dragged it before Chemosh in Qeriyyoth. And I settled therein the men of SHRN, and the men of MḤRTH. And Chemosh said unto me, 'Go, take Nebo against Israel.' And I went by night, and fought against it from the break of dawn until noon. And I took it and slew the whole of it, 7000 men and . . . , and women and . . . and maid-servants; for I had devoted it to 'Ashtor-Chemosh. And I took thence the vessels of Yahweh, and I dragged them before Chemosh. And the king of Israel had built Yahaz, and abode in it, while he fought against me. But Chemosh drave him out from before me."

In estimating the similarity in the matter of religious thought and sentiment between this inscription of the Moabite king and the early historical sources of the Hebrews, it must be remembered, when the latter are read in the authorized or revised versions, that the Hebrew proper name Jehovah (strictly, as in the inscription above, Yahweh) is replaced by the common title Lord. In this way many passages in the English version lose much of their point; this is particularly the case where, as *e.g.*, in Judges xi. 23 f., Jehovah and another god are brought into connection with one another.

www.ingramcontent.com/pod-product-compliance
Lightning Source LLC
Chambersburg PA
CBHW071623170426
43195CB00038B/2085